COMING OUT TO GOD

ALSO BY CHRIS GLASER

Uncommon Calling: A Gay Man's Struggle to
   Serve the Church

Come Home! Reclaiming Spirituality and
   Community as Gay Men and Lesbians

Prayers
for
Lesbians
and
Gay Men,
Their
Families
and
Friends

COMING

OUT

TO

GOD

CHRIS GLASER

WESTMINSTER / JOHN KNOX PRESS
Louisville, Kentucky

Scripture quotations unless otherwise noted are from
the Revised Standard Version of the Bible and are
copyrighted 1946, 1952, © 1971, 1973 by the
Division of Christian Education of the National Council
of the Churches of Christ in the U.S.A. and are used by
permission. In some instances, adaptations have been
made for the sake of inclusive language.

Scripture quotations marked JB are from *The Jerusalem
Bible,* copyright © 1966, 1967, 1968 by Darton,
Longman & Todd, Ltd., and Doubleday and Co., Inc.
Used by permission of the publishers.

Cover and interior illustrations by Michael Christman

Book design by Publishers' WorkGroup

First edition

Published by Westminster/John Knox Press
Louisville, Kentucky

PRINTED IN THE UNITED STATES OF AMERICA

9 8 7 6 5 4 3

Library of Congress Cataloging-in-Publication Data

Glaser, Chris.
 Coming out to God : prayers for lesbians and gay
men, their families and friends / Chris Glaser. — 1st
ed.
        p.   cm.
 Includes index.
 ISBN 0-664-25176-5

 1. Gays—Prayer-books and devotions—English.   2.
Devotional calendars.
 I. Title.
 BV4596.G38G58 1991
 242'.8'008664—dc20   90-24231

Dedicated to friends
who have lived with AIDS
who live with AIDS and ARC
and who live with HIV

Andy, Andrew
Bert, Bill, Bill, Billy, Bob
Carter, Charles, Chris, Christopher, Clyde,
Craig
Dave, David, David, David, David, Dick,
Don, Douglas
Ed, Ed
Gary, George, Greg
Howard
James, Jeff, Jim, Jim, Jim, John, John, John,
John, Justin
Ken, Ken, Kevin
Larry, Larry, Les, Luis, Lyle
Mark, Matthew, Michael
Nicholas
Peter
Richard, Rodger, Ron, Ron, Ron, Ron, Roy
Scott, Stan, Steve
Terry, Tim, Tom
William

For others unknown to me
or for whom memory fails
and for others I've simply met or known
All cherished by God

CONTENTS

Contents

PART III: Citizens of a Commonwealth   117

ACKNOWLEDGMENTS

These prayers evolved from my experience of the always-present and yet ever-growing spiritual awareness of the lesbian and gay community. I believe that our community includes our families (biological and chosen) and our friends (personal, political, and ecclesiastical). I am profoundly grateful to God for this community of nurture, of challenge, and of vision. I also thank God for opportunities and abilities to express our spirituality.

Particularly, I express gratitude for the Lazarus Project of the West Hollywood Presbyterian Church and Presbyterians for Lesbian & Gay Concerns of the Presbyterian Church (U.S.A.) for embodying God's love for me. Within these communities, my prayers found voice.

I thank those who read my manuscript and offered invaluable insights and corrections: Reverend Lisa Bove, a pastor and friend; Pat Hoffman, a close friend and author of *Ministry of the Dis-*

possessed, describing the ministry of the farm worker's movement; and George Lynch, D.Min., my lover and friend.

Though rewritten or recast here, some of these prayers found their way to this volume after publication in other prayer books I have written. I would like to thank the editor of the *More Light Update,* James D. Anderson, and the executive board of Presbyterians for Lesbian & Gay Concerns for their support of my annual *More Light Prayer Books.* I would also like to thank the board of governors of the Lazarus Project for the initial printing of *Prayers for Lent.*

I am grateful for the enthusiastic response of the editorial board and staff of Westminster/John Knox Press to this book of prayers. Especially I thank my editor, Alexa Smith, M.Div., for encouraging my writing and helping shape this book. Thanks, too, to copyeditor Esther Kolb for making helpful suggestions. It's also a pleasure to work with my friend Michael Christman, the talented graphic artist who designed the cover and created the illustrations.

Most of all, I thank you who pray with me by reading *Coming Out to God.* I thank God for you all, and I thank you all for my fuller experience of God.

C.R.G.
West Hollywood, California

INTRODUCTION

At the strict, fundamentalist Christian school I attended as a child, a teacher's fingers were noticed dancing to music from the radio. Another teacher remarked, "God's going to let you dance in heaven!" And I wondered, why was dancing permissible in heaven, but not on earth? Later I would learn it was because dancing was associated with sexuality, and sexuality was viewed as the enemy of spirituality.

The prophet Miriam led women in a dance celebrating God's deliverance of her people from Pharaoh's armies. King David danced almost naked in the religious procession bringing the Ark of the Covenant into Jerusalem. Yet many people today forget that dance was integral to early religious ritual. The body was not originally confined in worship to sitting, standing, and kneeling, as in most churches today. Worship was an invitation to dance, in celebration and in service. Worship was a bodily and sensual experience, not simply an act of mind or spirit. And that which was done by the body—in worship and otherwise—had spiritual implications.

Sexuality and spirituality are not opposing forces, as is frequently supposed today. Instead, both draw people into relationship. Sexuality draws us into physical relationships: touching, hugging, holding, caressing, and, most intimately as lovers, kissing and intercourse. Spirituality draws us into relationships that both include and transcend bodies because it includes and transcends that which is visible. These relationships are found in worship, service, commitment, political action, and, most intimately, in prayer and meditation. Both our sexual and spiritual powers are holy, and therefore both may be profaned. At their holiest, these powers lead to love in all its many expressions. At their most profane, they may lead to apathy or hate. The integrity of both sexual and spiritual powers is called the soul.

Christianity sanctifies both body (the visible experience) and spirit (the invisible experience) clearly by its single most revolutionary theological assertion: God's "Word became flesh" (John 1:14). For Christians, even God's Spirit is embodied—not only in Jesus Christ, but in all who do God's will (Acts 10:34–48).

I view these two powers, my sexuality and my spirituality, as dancers. Initially both were wallflowers, afraid to dance. My spirituality was immobilized by proscriptions and fixed answers. My sexuality was hiding in a closet, ashamed of itself.

When my sexuality began to emerge, my spirituality froze in fear, then nearly ran out of the room. But then it noticed other souls dancing gracefully, and realized it was missing their grace. My spirituality wondered if the lack of grace had something to do with rejection of the stranger on the other side of the room, my sexuality.

Timidly, one invited the other to dance. At first, they never looked at each other, out of embarrassment, shyness, perhaps even contempt. They were lousy dancers. Then they cast furtive glances toward each other, sometimes angry or resentful, sometimes flirtatious and seductive. Each took turns attempting to lead, to control the dance, while the other felt crowded and claustrophobic and backed away. Finally they found times when the dance led *them,* and for brief moments they became perfect dancers, full of grace, true to each other. They danced together as my soul.

Nowadays I feel awkward when either of them, my sexuality or my spirituality, seizes control of my dance to the detriment of the other.

For most of us, our spirituality dances awkwardly with our sexuality, if at all. Because we are taught that sexuality and spirituality are opposing forces, we either allow our spirituality to intimidate or dominate our sexuality, or we ignore our spirituality to enjoy our sexuality, or we do a little bit of both (compartmentalizing). Homophobic religions and heterosexist traditions try to prevent lesbians and gay men from dancing out our sexuality in the context of our faiths. An erotophobic

Introduction

religious tradition restricts homosexual, bisexual, and heterosexual alike from celebrating their sexual natures. A churchphobic gay or feminist community and a secularized world may limit our celebration of our spiritual natures.

Yet in Christian tradition there have been moments of insight that serve as correction to the tendency to separate sexuality and spirituality. In the late fourteenth century, Julian of Norwich wrote, "Our sensuality is grounded in Nature, in Compassion, and in Grace. . . . In our sensuality, God is. . . . God is the means whereby our Substance and our Sensuality are kept together so as never to be apart" (*Meditations with Julian of Norwich*; Santa Fe, N. Mex.: Bear & Co., 1986; pp. 92, 95). This nun (who would later be acclaimed a saint) affirmed that God may be found within our sensual experience, and that in God our Substance (essence) and our Sensuality (embodiment) are one.

In prayer, coming out to God as sexual-spiritual beings opens us up, I believe, to *God coming out to us* in the dance of Substance and Sensuality, spirituality and sexuality. Prayer becomes a place wherein the choreography of the dance of spirituality and sexuality gets worked out. When we allow the Lord of the Dance to lead, sexuality becomes responsible and spirituality becomes responsive. Sexuality becomes responsible by becoming centered ("grounded in Nature, in Compassion, and in Grace"), and spirituality becomes responsive by becoming embodied.

I believe that the gracefulness of our dance, a gift of God as Sovereign of our dance, arises from an integrity of sexuality and spirituality. One cannot idolize nor idle-ize the other; both dance together as soul. And why can't we dance on earth as in heaven?

Sexuality and spirituality enjoy a profound and an intimate connection because both find their source and their strength in the love known by the Greeks as *erōs*. As James B. Nelson explains it in his book *The Intimate Connection: Male Sexuality, Masculine Spirituality* (Westminster Press, 1988):

> Eros is desire. It is the quest for fulfillment through communion with the object of our love. That which we need, which we seek, might be another person. It also might be art, music, nature, God, or countless other sources of attraction. We experience eros when we are drawn to another, when we strongly sense the other's attraction, when we find ourselves both filled and filling in communion with the other. Eros is sensuous and bodily. It has strong emotions. We want to touch, to feel, to experience the other. (P. 54)

> Eros is longing. At its deepest it is the urgent longing of our whole being for communion and connectedness. Communion is holy. (P. 55)

And in her book *WomanChrist: A New Vision of Feminist Spirituality* (Harper & Row, 1987), Christin Lore Weber writes:

> Eros is yearning. He is desire. Paul Tillich associates eros with our passion for meaning and value. And

Introduction

> St. Augustine identifies eros as the power that impels us toward God. The loss of eros, and one's resignation to that loss, leaves a person passionless, sterile, without vision of possibilities, empty of meaning and value for life, and with a conviction of powerlessness to change one's situation. (Pp. 86–87)

It is precisely this profound and intimate connection between spirituality and sexuality that causes many religious people problems. There is a fear that sexuality will get out of control: how often have gay people been told that acceptance of homosexuality would open a Pandora's box of unwanted sexual expression? There is a fear that if sexuality were not strictly controlled, spirituality would suffer. This may be the root of the notion that they are opposing forces. So the answer is for spirituality to control sexuality. This has usually taken the form of suppression.

Yet the nature of eros, the source and strength of both spirituality and sexuality, encourages a loosening of control. In the following quote Nelson speaks of male experience, but because I believe that what he describes increasingly applies to women as well as men I have used inclusive language:

> [Eros] encourages [us] to loosen [our] grip on the need to control, and that is both its attraction and its fearfulness. . . . Still, eros draws us. Sometimes it appears through epithymia, flesh's longing for flesh, and should that loving result in orgasm, for a delicious moment we are thrown out of control. It is the experience [we] both seek and fear. It is true of

intimacy in general. Intimacy does not thrive on patterns of control. It does thrive when control needs are relaxed, when deep desire for connection is admitted. That is an invitation to the holy. (Pp. 55–56)

Prayer is such an invitation to the holy. As with other intimate activities, it thrives when we relax our controls and admit our desire for true connection and communion, intimacy and integrity—with the Creator, with creation, with fellow creatures. And it is in these relationships that we may discover and celebrate ourselves as the children of the cosmos, of God, that we are.

Those of us who have left religious institutions because of our sexuality have sometimes understood ourselves as rejecting or ignoring spirituality. But we are spiritual people nonetheless. We believe in *something* that keeps us going. This is especially evident in how most of us have coped with AIDS. Our anger, our fear, our compassion, our love—all reveal our relatedness and our desire for relationship with one another and the world in which we live. They reveal our innate spirituality.

A prayer life is simply an intentional way of recovering an awareness of our spirituality. Prayer is our dialogue with God, with the cosmos, with our truest selves. In prayer and meditation, our passion and purpose and values surface. Now that we are beginning to affirm who we are in other areas of our experience—whether as gay

Introduction

or lesbian or as one who loves someone who is gay or lesbian—why not affirm ourselves within the context of spirituality? Why not affirm ourselves by coming out to God? Taking time for exploration of the "child of the universe" within ourselves and reaching beyond ourselves to community, creation, and Creator offer spiritual pleasure: We enjoy who we are; we recognize the spiritual dimensions of our sexuality and sexual expression (as well as the spiritual dimensions of our sexual oppression); we find spiritual community with those with whom we share mutual support and valuing; we discover community with others who are marginalized; we view the creation with renewed awe and wonder; and we discover a God who gives us life and unconditional love.

My prayer life is the principal sustaining factor in my own ability to survive the homophobia of society, as well as to serve as an activist for the acceptance of lesbian women and gay men in church and culture. It has offered me both communion and sanctuary, at first in the loneliness of the closet, then in the challenges of reaching out for love and community among other gays and lesbians. As I enjoyed receiving and expressing love and being out of the closet, prayer served as my offering of much joy and many thanksgivings. And now, facing HIV infection and AIDS among my friends and within my community, prayer is the altar on which I may lay all my fears, anxieties, grief, anger, and despair, while receiving compassion, love, joy, and peace.

Prayers grow out of both personal and communal understandings of the nature of God, the cosmos, and humanity. While I do not share all the beliefs of my Christian sisters and brothers, my prayers grow out of my own Christian understanding. My prayers emerge from Christian perspectives, thought processes, language, and imagery. I do not claim Christian spirituality encompasses all truth or the only truth. In my prayer life I also use devotional material from other faith perspectives. That's why I believe that the prayers offered in this book may enrich anyone's prayer life, whatever their faith. And, since much of civilization is influenced by Jewish and Christian thought, many more who do not consider themselves religious will readily comprehend the meaning of these prayers.

Praying publicly is not one of my favorite activities, because it seems presumptuous, outwardly pious, and inevitably self-conscious. It is also extremely intimate: first, because revealing our spirituality is probably the final frontier of intimacy; and second, because praying honestly and with integrity welcomes disclosures we might prefer not to make. If I hesitate to pray publicly, why, then, do I make this offering?

What I have learned about myself in recent years is that my writing is a form of prayer. It brings me into communion with God, with oth-

Introduction

ers, and with myself. It welcomes the integrity of
sexuality and spirituality, intuition and reason,
learned technique and spontaneous creativity,
pleasure and work. Writing often provides a sense
of exquisite fulfillment for me, as do, for example,
my morning prayers or my opportunities for lovemaking. And the reason all of these may be so
fulfilling is that each is an opportunity to feel intimately connected to another, which is, I believe,
the goal and the gift of both spirituality and sexuality. I say both goal and gift because an intimate
connection is something to move toward, yet it is
always a gracious gift. It's like walking toward a
present, picking it up, unwrapping it, and welcoming it by giving thanks. An intimate connection spiritually and/or sexually requires our
participation, but it is no less a gift.

You can begin to understand, then, why I join
sexuality and spirituality in my work with words,
in that all three afford intimate connections. To
write prayers reflecting on spirituality and sexuality becomes a triple blessing. I find writing
prayers healing, life-giving, growth-producing,
community-building, and peace-making. My hope
is that reading them might do the same for you.
Perhaps you will discover unspoken prayers of
your own heart verbalized in them. Maybe they
will prod you to pray for yourself. At the least I
hope that reading them will direct your attention
to yourself, your faith, your community, and your
God for a few minutes a day. Though written out
of the experience of lesbians, gays, and those close

to us, many deal with issues common to all, such as self-esteem, sexuality, social justice. Some of the prayers may not specifically mention lesbians and gay men, yet deal with concerns familiar to us. Sometimes they include statements that God seems to be making in scripture; sometimes they include my own personal reflections on a subject that I feel like expressing aloud—to God, to anyone who reads this book. The sentences of the prayers have been broken into fragments, not out of poetic pretensions, but to slow the reader for meditation.

These prayers will aid you spiritually only if the Spirit and you enable them to do so. The most profound words in the world will not touch your heart without your assent and the Spirit's presence; on the other hand, the least profound words may, with your and the Spirit's cooperation. Reformed theologian John Calvin did not believe that the worthiness of the minister affected the validity of the sacrament. By extrapolation, neither my worthiness, your worthiness, nor the worthiness of these words will affect this sacrament of prayer if your heart is open and the Spirit is present. The spiritual life is an interplay of discipline and grace: our discipline, that is, taking the time to pray regularly; and God's grace, that is, God's unearned favor, mercy, and love. Since God's grace is always available, the responsibility is upon us to make ourselves accessible through the discipline of prayer.

Within the context of this discussion on the

merits of words, I must affirm my need, for spiritual reasons, to use language that includes both male and female, in relation both to ourselves and to God. Long ago, I recognized my need to address God as both Mother and Father, in the prayer Jesus taught us and elsewhere. Using both images reflected more adequately the fullness of my experience of God. On the other hand, because I never associated the word God with gender, I have not found it helpful to address the Creator as "Goddess." For me, using the term Goddess encouraged hearing the term God as male. And I found myself agreeing linguistically with a female church member in the acting profession who preferred the term actor because actress sounded like "less." Too, goddesses in the Greek pantheon and in theologies of other cultures frequently played subservient roles to the male gods. So I chose to go in another direction by re-forming my understanding of God in female and male imagery. I also use other forms of address that are non–gender-specific. For those for whom my choices in this and other matters of language are spiritual stumbling blocks, I advise you to simply change the words to suit your own needs. That's what *I* do!

A caution: When you pray, remember that you are always praying as part of a broader spiritual community. In Christianity, we are reminded that we pray as part of the Body of Christ, the church. While prayer may be very personal, there is no such thing as "private" prayer. This understanding saves us from spiritual pride. We do not develop a "just-me-and-God" or "just-me-and-Jesus" mentality that separates rather than unites us to other Christians and other people of faith. We contribute not only to ourselves but to the whole spiritual community with our prayer life. When praying these or other prayers, we pray with and for others as well as ourselves. If you don't identify with a need, doubt, or thanksgiving expressed in a written prayer, remember that you can be praying for someone else who has that need, doubt, or thanksgiving.

Though connecting us to countless saints, seen and unseen, in all times and places, the intimacy possible in prayer is profound. Even the Lord's Prayer as we know it is begun too formally. Jesus addressed God with a more intimate and affectionate term than "Father," a word more closely translated "Daddy." Popular belief and practice notwithstanding, prayer may be as intimate as or more so than other forms of intimacy. Even false or flowery words cannot hide the heart (in Jesus' day, the seat of the will), which is naked in God's eyes. The more our words adequately reflect the meditation of our hearts (whether confessing, doubting, questioning, affirming, or giving thanks), the more at one we are with ourselves, with God, and with others. Prayer may become an expression of our integrity. Our hearts, willing or not, are always within God's embrace. Prayer is, in a sense, our assent to God's desire for spiritual lovemaking.

Introduction

So let us enjoy our spiritual as well as our sexual lovemaking and the intimacy and integrity
they may afford us, for, thereby, we are reminded
that we belong in God's world: created in God's
image, called for community, and citizens of a
spiritual commonwealth.

PART
I

CREATED IN
GOD'S IMAGE

According to the Jewish creation stories found in Genesis, we are created in God's image. That means, among other things, that we are spiritual creatures. But what does that mean? What is spirituality? Simply described, spirituality is that invisible connection we experience with people, the cosmos, and sometimes a Higher Power, Divine Spirit, or God. Spirituality also consists of those intentional relationships among creatures, creation, and Creator which fuel our passion and give our lives meaning and purpose. Often communities or cultures experience connection and relationship and meaning in similar ways, and this gives rise to religions. To protect the sacred purposes of religion, religious institutions are formed.

Most of us have had at least some negative experiences with religious institutions. Sometimes we have experienced them as unhealthy, demanding, and manipulative in their need for control of our lives. Confirmation in the faith has meant "conformation." Sometimes we have witnessed them behaving as dysfunctional families: dysfunctional in their inability to speak honestly about sexuality and fairly about homosexuality and to positively integrate both within the schema of spirituality. Sometimes we have been shamed by religious institutions for who we are or how we express our feelings, thus weakening our self-esteem.

These experiences contradict the nature of spirituality. Spirituality is not about control, or dishonesty, or rejection of human experience, or an inability to deal with reality, or the destruction of self-worth. Clearly, then, homophobia and heterosexism contradict the nature of spirituality. Spirituality is about acceptance, honesty, integrity, living in the real world, and the valuing of ourselves and others. So self-affirming lesbians and gays and gay-affirming friends and family reflect the intent of spirituality. Spirituality means liberation for gays and lesbians from the Levitical-Pauline shackles forged for us by a prejudiced church as well as recovery of our original blessings, made in God's image.

In 1978, the Presbyterian Church dealt a devastating blow to its lesbian and gay members, their families, friends, and supporters. While calling for gay civil rights, and "welcoming" gay people as church members, the church voted against our ecclesiastical rights, denying lesbians and gays the opportunity to be ordained as ministers, elders, and deacons. That year, the church also refused to receive the annual report of Presbyterians for Lesbian & Gay Concerns.

I had been deeply involved in the nationwide debate on the ordination of "self-affirming, practicing homosexuals." I was one of the gay candidates seeking ordination as a minister. I served on the Task Force to Study Homosexuality, whose majority report recommended that the church should not consider homosexuality a bar to ordination. I had become coordinator of Presbyterians for Lesbian & Gay Concerns, edited their newsletter, and authored the annual report that

Created in God's Image

was rejected. I directed a church-sponsored ministry of reconciliation within the gay and lesbian
community in West Hollywood, California, called
the Lazarus Project, named for the one Jesus
called from death to life, out of a closet-tomb.
Much of my identity, as perceived by others, was
related to my sexuality.

A few weeks after the negative pronounce-
ment, a friend decided I needed to get away and
took me to Aspen, Colorado. Aspen in the sum-
mertime is fresh and green and Edenlike. Alone
with myself, I climbed a small mountain. As I did
so, I felt my soul undressing, removing the man-
tles that hung heavy on my shoulders. I was no
longer gay; I was no longer Presbyterian; I was no
longer male; I was no longer Christian. As I un-
burdened myself of these identities, my soul
soared as my body ascended. What a relief! I
sighed. What a release! I felt that I was getting in
touch with a deeper, unjudged self. The natural
surroundings seemed to welcome my naked soul.

And then, as if all of this were not enough, I
made a serendipitous discovery. At the top of the
mountain that I climbed was a grassy meadow,
surrounded by aspens whose fresh, silver-green
leaves flickered in the wind as candle flames in a
sanctuary. I laughed aloud, tears of joy sprang
from deep within me, and I danced ecstatically. I
rediscovered my original blessing as a child of
God, created in God's image. Now my identities
were placed in a broader, if not cosmic, perspec-

tive. The God of this sanctuary required nothing, but offered me all the joy and peace and love I needed.

Many if not most of us have, at one time or another, happened onto "meadows" where we have serendipitously felt welcomed by something or someone greater than ourselves and experienced divine joy. We all have had experiences of grace. Perhaps it was in the arms of a lover. Maybe it was singing the Hallelujah Chorus from Handel's *Messiah.* It might have been rafting down a river, writing a poem, or enjoying a wonderful Thanksgiving dinner with family or friends. Perhaps it was volunteering as a buddy with a person with AIDS, or working for a just political cause, or simply "being there" for a friend who needed us. All of these may serve as "icons" or "sacraments" revealing our true worth and God's loving presence.

Prayer may serve as another icon or sacrament of our true worth and of God's loving presence. Prayer is an opportunity to look within our life experience to find meaning and hope. It may become the meadow wherein we laugh and cry and dance. It may become the place above the mountain of perceptions, expectations, agendas, and struggles of everyday life, a place where we enjoy our divine worth as children of God and as an integral part of the cosmos.

Late in his ministry, Jesus took a few disciples to a mountaintop where, in prayer, they saw him transfigured, witnessed him commune with saints of the past, and heard God's voice from a cloud saying, "This is my Son, my Chosen; listen to him!" (Luke 9:28–36).

For us as well, prayer may be a place where we are transfigured and transformed. It may provide opportunities to commune with saints of the past and present, with saints all around the globe, with saints of all faiths. There God can meet us, and affirm, "This is my beloved child." Prayer awaits us whenever we need to restore our souls, regain our perspective, and renew our vision. Prayer is the place wherein our deeper identities are revealed, and we, in a sense, meet and take joy in our selves, created in God's image.

DAY 1

God,
the earliest Gospel writer
wastes no time informing us
that Jesus rose early
and found a lonely place
to pray.

God, the closet is already a lonely place,
but the point is well taken.

Those of us in closets
may use our wilderness experience
as an opportunity for prayer.

Those of us out of closets
may escape the pressure—and the glory—
that freedom in promised lands entails
by taking time to be with you.

In prayer, the closet doors open
between the human and the divine,
between those who are gay
    and those who are not,
between those in the closet and out.

Thank you, God, for opening doors
in the midst of dividing walls,
making us one Body
as we pray together.

Thank you, God, for opening doors
to your divine glory,
and the divine glory within us,
illuminating our darkest closet,
casting in shadow our brightest revelations.

Thank you, God, for opening doors among us,
though we are separated
geographically, culturally, ethnically,
      sexually,
that we might pray as one community,
transcending our own Diaspora,
our own dispersion among those
who do not share our experience,
either of spirituality or of sexuality.

In prayer,
you have made all ground between us
holy ground.
We remove our shoes in reverence.

DAY 2

O Holy One,
forgive me for seeking
embraces from others
before seeking the embrace
    you so readily offer.

There are days, Holy One,
when I don't want to talk to you.
I run from your presence,
finding distractions
to keep me from looking into your eyes.
No time at work today, and tonight—
laundry, a meeting,
a nightcap with a friend.

But, damn!
When I do lift my downward gaze
you're inevitably there with smiling eyes,
a steadfast, loyal friend
    wanting the best for me.
Why don't I want the best for myself?
Like Martha, I'm busy in the kitchen,
envious of Mary sitting at your feet,
choosing the better portion.
What's keeping me
from the better portion?

I am so busy with others' agendas
or my agenda
that I fail to discover
what *your* agenda may be.
Providentially,
I have caught glimpses of your will for me

despite myself and my crowded life.
Now I come out
to the full, abundant life you offer
as I follow your call.
Sorry you had to shout!

May I listen more carefully
to the nuances of this call.

DAY 3

Most intimate Friend,
the church says no to homosexuality
        in any form
while my body seems to say yes to it
        in every form,
and my soul cautions
        there must be a middle way.
Why do I let either the church
        or my sexual urges
distract me from an integrity
        of sex and spirit?

How I delight in the sensual dance!
—the delicious intimacy of letting go,
being open and vulnerable and embraced.

Yet there's something fearsome about it:
I don't want to entirely lose *me* in the dance,
nor *you,* God.

" 'All things are lawful,'
but not all things are helpful."
The apostle Paul is so right, God!

But why does your church so frequently
make sexuality a seductive enemy,
and spirituality a frigid expression?

If we could let go of our need for control,
if we could let our guard down a little,
we might delight in the delicious intimacy
of the body's spiritual/sensual dance:
open and vulnerable, embracing one another,
within you, the Holy Expanse of our dance.

God, teach me personally
    the delights of intimacy!
A friend, facing death, is learning to let go,
to let go of the need to take charge,
    to control.
May I, facing life, also learn to let go.
Lead me along the paths of intimacy—
ways to let go of my need to control
lover, family, friends,
even the church and the world.

O God, thy will be done.
Forgive me all that denies or betrays this.
So may I be forgiving,
for giving up control of others
and especially of you, God.

And may the church "let my people go"
to serve and praise you
in their dance of sense and spirit.

Amen.

DAY 4

Thank you for the body that loves me.

My own body:
it tingles me with pleasure
and sends pain as a warning;
it takes in food and air
and transforms them to life;
it reaches orgasmic bliss
and reveals depths of peace.

Thank you for the body that loves me.

My lover's body:
it surrounds me with safe arms,
and senses my needs and joys;
it allows me vulnerability,
and enables my ecstasy;
it teaches me how to love
and touches me with love.

Thank you for the body that loves me.

My spiritual community's body:
it embodies your presence
by embracing mine;
it incarnates your hope
by empowering prophets;
it inspires me with stories
and enchants me with mystery.

Thank you for the body that loves me.

The cosmic and mystical body:
it calls me to communion

with creatures and creation;
it manifests your glory
and mine as its child;
it upholds my feet
and heals my body.

Thank you for the body that loves me.

DAY 5

Dear God,
why am I anxious?

I remember Jesus said
anxiety cannot add to the span of life.
Doctors today say, in fact, it shortens life.
And my own experience of anxiety is
    that it feels
as if my chest is being squeezed too tightly,
my very life being pressed out of me.

A media report indicates anxiety about AIDS
may perversely increase careless sexual
    encounters.
Suicide has been used before
    to escape anxiety—
the feeling of "Let's get it over with."
And, as I observe the hard living
still going on in the gay community,
I can't help but wonder
    if that attitude is not present.

Yet, why do we so easily condemn
    a suicidal tendency
when it involves drugs, alcohol, and sex,
and ignore the suicidal attitude inherent in
    workaholism, repressed sexuality,
        and production of toxic waste?
I don't like living in anxiety.
But it's preferable to suicidal solutions.

O God,
may I receive your gift of a prayer life

as a life-giving
rather than life-surrendering
way of dealing with anxiety.
Enable me to find
the deep, still water beneath,
far below the troubled surface.

DAY 6

Giver of grace and love and joy:
I wish I could discipline my prayer life
to receive your gifts
as easily as I am able to regularize
other areas of my life
to receive what they offer.

I can organize my work schedule
to accomplish much
and earn an income.

I can make time for meals
—and, I confess, snacks—
and feed myself adequately.

I can find time three times a week
to work out one and a half hours at the gym,
making my body healthier
and more attractive.

But to find even half of an hour per week
to pray in solitude seems saintly!

Maybe the difference is that
work pays me,
food nourishes me,
and exercise improves
        my health and appearance.

There's no payoff in prayer—
or is there?
Meditation can't feed me—
or can it?

And no one notices
    when I've been working out spiritually.
Or do they?

I think I've answered my own questions, God.
Help me to remember
the reward and the nurture
I receive in prayer.
Help me to remember
how differently I treat myself and others
when I have been held in your loving embrace,
when I have held others in a loving prayer.

DAY 7

Jesus, there seems to be more mystery
in our music, in our art, in our films,
even on television,
than in our religion.
Why so much pragmatism
    in American religion, Lord?

"Make religion work for me," we cry to you.
"Make it practical."
"Make it useful."
A "show me" attitude toward your truth.
"Make me change."
"Make the world different."

Religion *can* work:
it *can* be practical, useful, demonstrable.
But, Jesus, your life reveals
    that religion is more—
it is faith,
and faith is ultimately mystery:
your faith worked
    when things didn't work out;
your faith was practically impractical;
your faith was usefully useless;
your faith was invisibly visionary.
Jesus, faith didn't save you from your Passion;
faith led you to an impractical conclusion—
government leaders
    saw no political value in it,
religious leaders
    envisioned no spiritual value.

Your Passion is mystery to us, Jesus,
but somehow we have been saved by it.
The symbol of your Passion, the cross,
has become a spiritual guidepost
ironically leading us from the ways of death
to the ways of choosing life.

Thank you, Jesus, for willing
to live and die for me,
to live and die for the world,
for no reason
but the passion of your love.

DAY 8

Divine Lover,
voices other than my own
dictate what is sin to me.
Yet much they label "sin"
my reason and my feelings
do not label so.
And much they consider innocent
my mind and my heart
find more abhorrent.

Why do I trust others' voices
rather than my own?
I fear my own delusion, yes,
but what of *theirs?*
Why do I consider *them* objective,
even in scripture?
Both scripture and society
have their own axes to grind.
Why should *I* be ground up with them?
As Paul reminds us,
if I partake with thankfulness,
why should I be bound
    by another's scruples?

Why is enjoying sexuality a sin?
And considered worse
    than wasting time or talent,
worse than acquisitiveness
    of things or power,
worse than betraying friendships,
or denying love?
Why do I give ear
to these stern taskmasters?

O Holy Lover,
bolster my self-trust,
increase my confidence in my perspective,
help me listen to the heart and mind
you have given me
as I follow the guidance of your Spirit,
as I learn from the Embodiment
        of your love for me.
Amen.

DAY 9

God, I believe
self-denial
may become
self-denying.

That virtue may become a vice
in which we are caught,
our life squeezed from us.

Such is not the saintliness you ask of us:
self-denial should never become self-denying,
but should rather lead to self-affirming,
affirming the soul, created in your image:
an integrity of body and spirit.

God of integrity,
lead me carefully along the narrow path
between human arrogance and pride
and self-negation.

Help me to ask my due.
Help me not to fear, or be nervous,
or apologetic, or self-deprecating.
Give me strength and power
to convince others of my just cause.
Keep me from being perceived as demanding,
but help me rather
    to be viewed as hopeful and worthy.
Teach me to receive in gratitude,
and feel affirmed
rather than embarrassed, ashamed,
    or unworthy.

God, from whose womb we are born
    and reborn,
you call us to be ourselves,
your children,
your image and essence,
your beauty.
Lead us toward the integrity and harmony
you enjoy in heaven and earth,
that we may share your commonwealth,
grace-fully-empowered.
Amen.

DAY 10

All-embracing Spirit,
I don't know what to say to you today.
It's like sharing a meal in silence
    with a friend,
or dropping wordlessly exhausted
    once home from work.

I do not believe
I will be saved by my words,
though I usually feel compelled
to say them.

I do believe, God,
your grace is sufficient
to save me
even if I were silent.

I believe
I need times
to express your grace
in words.

I also believe
I need times
to experience your grace
in silence.

Intimate Spirit, today
I simply want to be in your presence.
Speak to me in this silence,
and let this silence speak to me.

DAY 11

Jesus, friend,
why do we associate physical beauty
    with moral good?
Why do we draw connections
    between spiritual worthiness
and mental and physical ability and prowess?
Why do we view material
    or vocational success
as an indicator of value?

Some of our best friends
are homely, not overly bright,
    hated gym class, are "unsuccessful."
Yet that doesn't overcome our prejudice.
We so easily can be conned
by a pretty face, a clever mind, a healthy body,
career or financial success—
either our own or others'.

But you can't be conned, Jesus.
You see to the heart of the matter.
You see to the heart of our matter.
You know if our heart
and the hearts of others
will what God wills.

No Gospel writer bothered
to write what you looked like,
or tell us your grades at yeshiva,
or describe your athletic trophies.
They spent more time writing
of your failure to communicate,
your ability to alienate when you *were* heard,

your ability to anger others
    even in doing good,
and your crucifixion
than they gave attention
    to your successful resurrection
(and they gave God the credit for that!).

Maybe your face was disfigured,
your physique distorted, your IQ low,
a ninety-eight-pound weakling
voted least likely to succeed.

Maybe your only saving grace
    (for you and for us)
was that your will coincided with God's,
having compassion on us
in our own suffering, our own weakness,
    our own failure,
as God does,
and yet always hoping the best for us.

DAY 12

Judge not, lest you be judged.

God of mercy,
I pray for healing for myself, for others,
afflicted by our anger at being misjudged,
wounded by our hurt over defeats,
exhausted from having to justify
    our presence.

My God, I believe
long before the world judges rightly,
long before we see victory,
long before explanations prove unnecessary,
that you will find creative purpose
    for our anger;
that you will tend and heal our wounds;
that you will give us rest and peace
    in your sacred arms.

Our enemies see things in black and white,
missing the spectrum of color.
My God, I thank you
that you do not judge in black and white.
Your rainbow promises
a multicolored perspective
    of merciful discernment.
You look in our hearts,
understanding our actions more tenderly
    than we do.

Judging ourselves too lowly
is as great a sin
as judging ourselves too highly.

And yet others judging us too lowly
can lead to our judging ourselves too highly,
a need to assert and affirm ourselves
        over others,
to their devaluation and to our discredit.

God, Lover of my soul,
I have done what you gave me to do—
However inadequately, forgive me.
However well, let me rejoice.
Lend your Spirit, God,
to lead me in discerning
when to confess
and when to rejoice.
Lead me from the precipice of false pride,
as well as the pit of false self-judgment.
Thank you for your loving judgment,
        forgiveness, and making anew.
Make me anew. Amen.

DAY 13

A lesbian friend of mine,
a minister,
wonders why you didn't send a woman
as your Child, God.

God, maybe you did,
and we missed her.
We might have been saved long before Jesus
    arrived on the scene,
if only our eyes and ears had been opened,
if only the demon of sexism
    had been cast out,
if only the pharisaic patriarchy's tables
    had been overturned.

But now that the Spirit
opens our eyes and ears,
helps us to recognize the evil of sexism,
and leads us toward
    an egalitarian commonwealth,
we have no excuse.

Lead us to attend, accept, and revere
your embodiment in women, Holy Creator.
Open us to affirm the feminine and masculine
of your embodiment within each of us,
    Holy Reconciler.

Touch us in people of all colors,
    ages, abilities,
and from all points on the Kinsey scale,
so we may be healed by your embodiment,
    Holy Spirit.

Then we will grasp
that you have come to us
many times over,
and we ignored or denied or betrayed
      your Content
because of its embodied form.

And wasn't that why Jesus of Nazareth
was ignored and denied and betrayed:
because we thought God's love
      could not be embodied
in a poor Jewish carpenter,
born of an unwed mother in lowly Bethlehem,
reared in the ghettos of Nazareth,
ministering in rural Galilee?

My friend's way of accepting
your sending a man
was to forgive and understand why.
This might lead us toward accepting
your various forms
by forgetting expectations
and asking ourselves, "Why not?"

DAY 14

O Power that is higher and holier,
sitting in my office this morning
I hear the almost overwhelming roar
    of traffic outside.
I find it threatening, disturbing my peace,
because it calls forth the roar,
    echoes the roar,
of the traffic inside my heart, my mind.
The traffic of fear and of busyness—
Will I get everything done today?
Will I stand approved for my efforts today?
Will I have been busy, efficient,
    and effective enough
to justify my salary
and the position
    with which I've been entrusted?

But the pressures I feel
are from myself and other human beings.
When can I let go of hands wrestling mine
and reach out for your hand alone?
When may I join you
in a leisurely walk through Eden again?

When I give myself permission.
When I let go,
when I shed the manipulations and desires
    of others and of my own ambitions,
recognizing my salvation does not lie
    with them,
but with you.

And your will for me,
in the words of the catechism,
is that I glorify you,
and enjoy you forever.

Beneath the myriad complexities
branching overhead in today's agenda,
may I walk peaceably with you.
Amen.

DAY 15

God of all ages,
why do I envy youth?
Have I forgotten my own youthful struggles,
my confusion, ignorance,
solutionless highs and lows,
naïveté, testing,
parental expectations,
peer pressure,
lack of independence?

Have I so soon forgotten
my uglifying acne,
my dread of gym class,
my loneliness and isolation as gay?

Young gay men and young lesbian women
must experience the same growing pains today.
Yes, things are more open for us,
but that doesn't mean their parents are,
or their peers.
It's still painful to be different.

God of all ages,
be present to lesbian and gay youth.
Coming out still means birth pain,
a grief process (letting go of other plans).
But it is the beginning of authentic life,
and didn't Jesus come also
        to bring authentic life?
Isn't that even now his passion?

Maybe it's the passion of youth I miss,
the freshness of vision,

the idealism,
the hope.
God of all ages,
restore to me the passion,
the freshness of vision,
the idealism and hope
that leads to authentic life.
In the name of its prime example,
Jesus Christ.

DAY 16

Dear Higher Power,
I failed last night.
I got crazy, crazy with rage, violent!

Today I try to discern
the source of this rage.
My inadequacy?
Another's inadequacy?
The *world's* inadequacy?

The message of "perfect"
still lingers within me:
"I can be . . . "
"I should be . . . "
"I will be . . . perfect."
Or,
"The world can be . . . "
"Another should be . . . "
"Life will be . . . perfect."

I cannot be perfect.
Neither can I expect that of the world,
or of another, or of life,
or perhaps even of you, Holy One.

Sometimes, in your sacred presence,
I feel perfection is attainable.
But it's not, so I return to you
to bask in the illusion.
But I don't want to become addicted
    to this illusion
any more than to the illusions of drugs,
    alcohol, or compulsive sexuality.

I want to stand in all humanness,
in imperfection,
incomplete,
struggling
at integration and integrity.
That is the human struggle.
I am human.
I am not God.

You who call all life into being,
you created me human,
not another god, not perfect.
Yet you have pronounced me,
with all creation, "good."
Lead me in paths of integrity.
Lead us all. Amen.

DAY 17

Mary,
you conceived more than a child.
You conceived a vision of God's intentions:
scattering the proud,
putting down the mighty,
exalting those of low degree,
feeding the hungry.

The Hannah of Jewish history
had also conceived the vision
in the birth of her child, Samuel:
that's why you sing her glorious psalm.
Elizabeth, your kin, did too, in John,
a conception that silenced her husband
but leapt at your good news.
And eighty-four-year-old Anna, the prophet,
fasting and praying, conceived it as well.

Mary,
your vision led you through
the pain of giving it birth,
the anguish and joy of assisting its growth.
It led you to the cross
And, finally, to an empty tomb.

Your vision has conceived more births,
more anguish and joy in growth,
more crosses,
and yet more empty tombs.

Your vision has
scattered the self-righteous,
brought down those who would judge,

exalted the marginalized,
and nourished us with hope.

As we conceive your vision
        in our own communities,
may we remember those who have gone before
        us in the dream,
and may we also be blessed with kin
        who greet us with joy,
and prophetic voices who offer thanks to God.

Our soul magnifies our God,
our spirit rejoices in God our deliverer,
for God has regarded our oppression.
Generations to come will call us blessed,
for God has done great things for us,
and holy is God's name.

DAY 18

Holy One who knows my heart:
why do I do the very thing I wish to avoid?
What are these compulsions within me
that sometimes strangle my will?
The apostle Paul shared this problem.
How did he overcome it? Or did he?
I know what is best for me,
and yet something inside me jumps up,
wanting to do something other,
sabotaging my good intent.

Did Jesus struggle too?
Did he struggle to do what was best for him
and therefore for the world?
His Passion is presented pretty much
    as a *fait accompli*
long before he pronounced
    his mission accomplished.
Why, then, did he apparently overreact,
angrily denouncing Peter
    ("Get behind me, Satan!")
when Peter innocently protested
his prophecy of suffering
as they approached Jerusalem?
And what about his turning over the tables
    in the Temple?
Was he fearful that his own worship of you
might become cluttered with the commerce
    of the world, too?
And I doubt that his temptations were limited
    to his forty-day fast in the wilderness—

these must represent temptations
    throughout his ministry.

We've made Jesus so godly, God,
we forget your intent in joining us
    in the flesh—
to become so human, God,
that you struggled alongside us,
tempted in every way as we are.

You must know what it's like for me, then,
doing the very thing I wish not to do.
Immanuel, God-with-us, means
God-struggles-with-us.
Thank you, God, for being a fellow struggler,
instead of an impossible ideal.

DAY 19

Great Spirit,
why do I keep myself
from your holy sanctuaries:
the hugs of ones who love me,
the inspiration of true fulfillment,
the grace of natural beauty,
the embrace of spiritual
     community?

Open my heart
that I may recognize these places
of healing, of wholeness,
of integrity, of growth
for me.

Help me to transform
or, if need be, abandon
sources of alienation:
bad relationships,
unfulfilling activities,
unhealthy environments,
unsupportive community.

Open my eyes
that I may recognize places
of wounding, of brokenness,
of segregation, of stagnation
for me.

As I walk through the valley
of these shadows of death,

lead me to the green pastures
beside still waters
by which you restore my soul.
Amen.

DAY 20

O God,
I lack a certain courage:
to risk abandoning all my closets
to fulfill life's dreams,
giving up securities, pretensions,
presumptions, indulgences,
fears—especially fears—
to be all you claim I am,
to be all you call me to be,
to be all you hope for me.

I dawdle at the starting line,
telling myself I'll begin tomorrow.
Or, part way through the race,
I decide, I deserve a break today,
and find it difficult to limit that break
to time enough to rest and restore myself
to run again.

Dear God,
Jesus fought the good fight,
finished his race,
and kept faith with his dreams
of your commonwealth.

Why do you give me this model, God?
It's like comparing my body
    to Arnold Schwarzenegger's,
or my ministry to Mother Teresa's,
or my sacrifice to martyred saints
    in Central America!

I can't give it all, can I, Lord?
I can't sacrifice all for the commonwealth of
      God, can I?

"Seek first God's kingdom . . . ,
and all these things shall be yours
      as well."

Jesus, is this true?
Did you have all you needed
as you gave everything to finish the race?

PART II

CALLED AS
COMMUNITY

A young sparrow flew against one of the glass walls of the campus chapel. The sanctuary must have seemed an open and inviting space, welcoming the bird's continued flight. But, the sparrow, abruptly halted by the nearly invisible glass, fell to the ground, badly injured. A student and I walked toward it to see if we could help. As we knelt on either side, all we could do was watch as it struggled for life and, finally, gave out its last breath. I buried it in the garden of the Religious Center of the University of Southern California, where I was serving as an interim chaplain.

Instantly, I felt overwhelmed by grief. But I hid my strong emotions at the small tragedy from the other campus chaplains and the staff and students gathered for lunch. Away from them, in the kitchen, as I washed the soil from the spoon I had used to dig the grave, an involuntary sob forced its way from deep inside me.

That very morning, I had found comfort in scripture for my grief over the many dimensions of the AIDS crisis. In the tenth chapter of Matthew, Jesus tells his disciples: "Do not be afraid of those who kill the body but cannot kill the soul. . . . Can you not buy two sparrows for a penny? And yet not one falls to the ground without God knowing. . . . So there is no need to be afraid; you are worth more than hundreds of sparrows" (Matt. 10:29–31, JB).

Now, having personally witnessed one of those sparrows fall, what comfort I had taken in Jesus' words seemed to dissipate. In the small, trembling body and agonized eyes of the sparrow, I saw a person with AIDS. In the tragic accident that led

75

to its downfall, that is, its mistaking glass walls of the chapel for open windows, I saw lesbian women and gay men mistakenly believing that the church might be open to them, only to be stopped violently by the invisible force of homophobia.

It is probably the helplessness and grief I feel over dearly loved friends who are infected by HIV, or who have AIDS, or who have died of AIDS, that gives a sense of urgency to my need to have my church welcome my people: lesbian women and gay men. I want my gay brothers to live long enough to see the Body of Christ throw open its arms and welcome them home. I want my lesbian sisters who suffer with us, as well as suffering the outrageous patriarchal sexism of the church, to survive long enough to witness the church's repentance and embrace.

My prayer life has, as a result, become more anguished and angry about the demonic forces within the church that paralyze that body's response. For me, AIDS anxiety has been overwhelmed by AIDS grief. Such grief triggers tears at any suffering I see. That's why the little bird's death moved me so deeply.

Gays and lesbians are also members of the Body of Christ. When we cry, Christ weeps, much as Jesus did for his beloved friend Lazarus. When we pray, Christ prays, much as Jesus prayed for unity among all who would be his followers. When we act, Christ acts, much as Jesus rebuked the self-righteous and healed the suffering. Our tears, our prayers, and our actions are God's. Our sensitivity, our spirituality, and our ministry are gifts of God's Spirit.

Having these gifts, let us use them. God knows and God feels the anguish, the pain, and the anger of our prayers as well as the joy and the gratitude we express. God knows and God feels the depths and the heights of the sexual and spiritual love that unites us. And God knows and God feels the healing our ministries bring, whether by prophetically challenging the comfortable or by pastorally comforting those who suffer.

Whether within or without the church, faithful lesbians and gays, along with those who love us, form a spiritual community. Praying with and for one another during personal or communal prayer, we become more fully aware of this spiritual community and of our collective passion and compassion. Lesbians and gay men can better listen to one another; families can increase their understanding of a lesbian or gay family member; we can better hear the concerns of our families and friends; gay and nongay friends can more adequately support one another; our advocates and our opposition may find common ground.

Jesus calls lesbian and gay Christians, our families, friends, and supporters into this community. Together, we may manifest the Body of Christ, who assures us all that "not [a sparrow] falls to the ground without God knowing. . . . So there is no need to be afraid; you are worth more" (JB).

DAY 21

Creator of justice!
Why do you create gay people
and then allow societal taboos to develop
     against us?

Why is there an ebb and flow
     to our acceptance?
Why are we more welcome
     in some periods of history
and some cultures of the world
and less welcome in others?
Are we "incidental suffering"
in your grand, creative experiment?
If a thousand years is like a day to you,
are a thousand suffering lesbians and gays
a drop in the cosmic bucket?

Thank you for Jesus,
evidence that you suffer with us—
the one or the many.
No pain, no tear,
no cross, no death
goes unnoticed.

Your compassion in Jesus Christ embraces
the lonely gay man in the bar,
the alienated lesbian woman in a marriage,
the person with AIDS losing energy and hope,
the closeted adolescent
     struggling with sexual identity,
and couples trying to love with few models
and relatively little societal support.

You know, God!
That's the story of the Christ:
you know and you care about each and all.
Christ's Passion is your passionate affair
     with us.
Who are we that you are mindful of us?
You have made us little less than you.
You have made us.
Thank you, God, for creating us!

DAY 22

Thank you, God, for our families.

Thank you for lesbian sisters
    and gay brothers
with whom we've worked and cried
    and laughed.

Thank you for lovers who live with us
and love us anyway.

Thank you for former lovers
    who've become friends
and friends who've become family.

Thank you for moms, dads, sisters, brothers,
sons, daughters, nephews, nieces,
aunts, uncles, grandmas, grandpas,
granddaughters, grandsons,
cousins, spouses, and in-laws
who have not stopped loving us
    because we're gay.

Thank you for our spiritual families:
congregations, support groups,
    Twelve-Step meetings,
lesbian and gay religious networks
    and chapters,
lesbian and gay choruses, bands, clubs,
    and athletic teams.

Thank you for our natural families:
our pets, our plants, our yards,
the shores, the parks, the forests.

Thank you for neighbors
        who welcome us into their homes
and strangers who smile at us.

Thank you for people who call
        to see how we're doing,
and people we may call
        to see how they're doing.

Thank you for people we know
        all over the globe,
people who've moved,
or whom we've left behind,
or whom we've met in transit.

Thank you for long-lost friends
who write us out of the blue.

Thank you for our very extended families
that expand our home beyond four walls.
Thank you for our gift of home-making:
offering and receiving hospitality
even in the midst
        of unwelcoming environments.
Thank you for blessing us
        with this special grace!
Alleluia! Amen!

DAY 23

Blessed are those aware
        of their spiritual needs,
  for theirs is the commonwealth of heaven.
Bless persons with AIDS and ARC
  and all who face life-threatening illness
  with a vision of their eternal worth.

Blessed are those who mourn,
  for they shall be comforted.
Bless those who grieve in the AIDS crisis
  over potential or actual loss:
  comfort lovers, parents, friends, families,
  and those who are infected with HIV.

Blessed are the meek,
  for they shall inherit the earth.
Bless those who are humbled
    by a positive HIV antibodies test
  with a fresh appreciation for their bodies
  and for the beauty of this world.

Blessed are those who hunger and thirst
    for righteousness,
  for they shall be satisfied.
Bless all who seek justice
  for persons living with AIDS:
    AIDS activists who,
  knowing that silence equals death,
  loudly demand adequate resources
    for research and care.

Blessed are the merciful,
  for they shall obtain mercy.

Bless all who seek cures and treatments,
  bless all who offer care,
  bless lovers, friends, and families
    who stand alongside,
  that they may be strengthened
    by your Spirit.

Blessed are the pure in heart,
  for they shall see God.
Bless all who seek their spirituality;
  may they find your Spirit
    within themselves,
  may they see you in the faces
    of those who love them,
  may they feel your healing touch
    in those who hold them.

Blessed are the peacemakers,
  for they shall be called children of God.
Bless all those who work to reconcile
    the church and society
  with the gay community,
  and with all the minorities
    affected by AIDS.

Blessed are those who are persecuted
    for righteousness' sake,
  for theirs is the commonwealth of heaven.
Bless those who would educate us all
    about AIDS,
  who confront fear with facts
  and challenge carelessness
    with confrontation.

Blessed are you when others revile you
    and persecute you
    and utter all kinds of evil against you
      falsely on my account.
Rejoice and be glad,
   for your reward is great in heaven,
   for so the prophets who were before you
     were persecuted.
Bless those who suffer rejection
   or discrimination
   due to AIDS and other disabling conditions,
   or due to AIDS activism
   and other enabling conditions:
   may their rights be protected here as in heaven.
   Amen.

(Beatitudes from Matthew 5:3-12)

DAY 24

Holy Trinity,
divine and blessed relationship,
bless the ecstasy of these lovers
as their faces kiss,
as their bodies touch,
as in their lovemaking
they overcome the fear and the hatred
and the garbage heaped upon them
by the church and the culture.

Bless their adoration of each other
as they worship the holy imprint
of your divine beauty
and enjoy the communion
of a loving covenant.
May such sacrament
bring them ever closer to you,
Lover of us all.

DAY 25

A priest sent a card
    of van Gogh's "Olive Orchard."
In the tortured brush strokes,
the artist reveals his own agony
as he depicts Christ's agony in Gethsemane.
The priest sees in the reproduction
his own spiritual struggle
    to accept his homosexuality.

Let us pray for this priest
    and the many like him
who are part of
    an invisible community of suffering,
unknown, unfelt, unloved by the church:

We pray, O God,
    for those who live in closets.

For the quarter of a million homosexuals
murdered in Nazi concentration camps
and those who remained imprisoned
    despite the Allied victory,
who now live in history's closet:

We pray, O God,
    for those who died in closets.

For millions of lesbians and gay men
    in other countries
in which there are
    no support systems or groups,
in which revelation leads to imprisonment,
    castration, or death:

We pray, O God,
    for those who fear in closets.

For priests, nuns, ministers,
    and lay church leaders
who, to serve the church, cannot come out,
while bringing liberation to others
    who are oppressed:

We pray, O God,
    for those who liberate from closets.

For spouses, who also must hide—
nongay spouses,
    protective of their loved ones' careers,
gay lovers,
    hiding their love under a bushel:

We pray, O God,
    for those who love in closets.

Thank you, God, for all who,
    throughout the world,
struggle to make churches and cultures
    more inclusive,
homes where there are no strangers:

O God,
may closets go the way of the Berlin Wall.
Alleluia! Amen.

DAY 26

Mother and Father of us all,
thank you for a church that welcomes me
    as I am.
There's something very comfortable
    and comforting
about being in our sanctuary.
Watching the deacons set up for Communion
is like watching family members set the table
for midday Sunday dinner at home.
The familiarity of the candles,
the cup and the bread, the flowers—
all offer a sense of home.

Dear God, being with you is being at home.
You, the forgiving father
who welcomes me at the door with a hug.
You, the nurturing mother
who holds me on her lap
and rocks me gently to sleep.

I feel safe.
I feel as if I belong.
Thank you, God.

I pray for lesbian and gay Christians
throughout the church
who need such a ministry of compassion,
    support, and advocacy,
but mostly get rejection and isolation.

Thank you, God, for exceptions:
for ministries and congregations
that welcome gay men and lesbian women

as full members of your community;
for support groups and networks
challenging the church to change
its Sodomlike inhospitality.

May all of these experience your Spirit
guiding them, embracing them,
nurturing them, and inspiring them
as they offer their ministries
and transform the church.

May the whole church follow their lead
welcoming lesbian and gay pilgrims home.

DAY 27

He's lonely, Jesus.
He's infected with HIV.
Though surrounded by friends,
he lives a lonely danger.
They can't truly share his fear.
Nor, should AIDS develop,
can they shoulder his grief.
And, if death comes,
he takes a solitary leap into the unknown.
And he wonders if you have abandoned him,
or worse, if he deserves your abandonment.

O Lord, hear his silent cries for help!
Bring healing to his soul!
After his weeping in the night,
bring him joy in the morning.
Transform his mourning into dancing.
How can he praise you
        from the pit of despair?
Lift him up to your mountain of hope,
that he may shout and sing
        of your faithfulness.

Jesus, he needs you.
You know the fear,
you bore the grief,
you took that solitary leap,
you also feared God's abandonment
("My God, why hast thou forsaken me?").
He needs to know that you're with him.
He needs to know that you're the ultimate
        AIDS Buddy.

Kiss him, Jesus,
kiss him deeply with your Spirit,
hold him to your breast,
heal his aloneness with your touch.

DAY 28

Thank you, Holy One, for this letter
of a gay woman thanking me
for helping her find her "voice"
    in the church.
But honestly, I needed her voice.
And you know it was not my faith
    but her faith
that made her whole:
her faith in you, divinely feminine;
her faith in your chosen ones: women
    of the Bible,
    of tradition,
    of the present faithful community;
her faith in herself,
    empowered by life and love,
    called by you
    for leadership and ministry.

O Holy One,
who unites the feminine and the masculine,
forgive me
for the patriarchal structures I enjoy
that push women away from such faith:
it would be better for patriarchies
if great millstones were hung
    round their necks
and thrown into the sea.

O Holy One,
forgive me
when I do not listen carefully to women
expressing their doubt and their faith:

for, hearing what must be questioned,
critiqued, or cast out
is as valuable as hearing
what faith may answer and affirm
      and accept.

O Holy One,
redeem us
with your Holy Spirit,
as she guides us into further truth
about your nature and our nature
and the nature of the commonwealth
you prepare for us
on earth as in heaven.

DAY 29

"What shall we do to inherit eternal life?"
"Go, sell your closets and follow me."

But, Jesus, we're rich in closets:
positions of prestige,
high-paying jobs,
families that offer security,
justice issues that require
        personal sacrifice,
expectations that we cannot disappoint.

"Think not that in the king's palace
        you will escape any more
        than all the other Jews. . . .
And who knows whether you have not come
        to the kingdom
        for such a time as this?"

Dear God, as a gay community we are divided
        by closets.
Some of us are not known as gay,
just as Esther was unknown to King Ahasuerus
        as a Jew.
Some of us find "grace and favor"
in the sight of those with power,
and are tempted as Esther to keep quiet,
even when our people are attacked.
As Esther risked her life in solidarity
        with her people,
celebrated now in the Jewish Festival
        of Purim,
open the eyes of us all to the solidarity
        needed

to protect the lives, rights, and livelihoods
    of our people.

Jesus, you told the young ruler
    wanting eternal life,
"Go, sell what you possess
    and give to the poor,"
and he went away sorrowful,
    for he was very rich.
Jesus, what would you say
    to your gay disciples?
"Go, sell your closets and give to the poor"
—the poor being other lesbians and gay men
with whom we avoid identifying
lest we become poor ourselves?

Deliver us, O God,
    from the rich young ruler's mistake.
Redeem us by the solidarity
    modeled in Esther.
May National Coming Out Day
    become our Purim.

DAY 30

There's a wall between us, God.
I love my friend,
but this isn't my friend.
He's on drugs and alcohol.
He's in another world
from which I feel shut out.
I want to be close,
I want to share feelings,
I want to laugh together,
I want to show my love,
but he's too intense one moment
and too distracted the next.

Dear God, why is the world in such a state
that escape seems necessary?
God, an altered state
makes us believe we're okay,
makes us feel divine,
makes us feel wonderful about our love
and our sexuality.

Dear God, why doesn't the church
help us believe these things?
Why doesn't the church
teach us that we're okay,
created in your image,
divinely gifted with our love
and our sexuality?

There's a wall between us, God.
I love the church,
but this isn't my church.
It's on dogma and legalism.

It's in another world,
from which I feel shut out.
I want to be close,
I want to share my feelings,
I want to laugh together,
I want to show my love,
but it's too intense one moment
and too distracted the next.

Yahweh, may this prayerful shout
help bring down Jericho walls
of drugs and dogma!
Amen.

Faithful God,
these parents watch anxiously for war news.
They worry that the government
will not act aggressively enough
to support the boys at the front.
Tens of thousands have lost their lives
    already.
A memorial is even now being pieced together.
And their son is on the front line
of the battle with AIDS.
He may only be at risk,
or he may be infected with HIV,
or he may have developed ARC or AIDS.
They worry. They love him.
They want him to be happy,
to enjoy love, to live a full life.

God, be with these faithful parents.
In the midst of too many unfaithful parents,
who have ignored, neglected, abandoned,
or rejected their gay and lesbian children,
these faithful, loving hearts
deserve your compassion and ours.
Battle-fatigued and war-weary,
they need your hope, God.
May their rage bring forth justice,
and may you grant them your peace.

And, God, what will become
of the veterans of this war?
What of the caregivers?
Not only mothers and fathers,

but lovers, brothers, sisters, friends,
AIDS volunteers and professionals?
And what of the survivors,
those gay men infected or uninfected?
Will they be treated like the veterans
of another unpopular war?
Who will cradle the lesbian
who cradled her buddy as he died?
Who will hold the terrorized gay man
who wakes from nightmares of suffering
        and death?

O God, why this suffering? Why this death?
O God, be with us in this wasteland.
Hold us, comfort us, touch us, heal us.
O Divine Comforter, wipe away every tear.

DAY 32

I saw him on the edge of the dance floor.
His eyes, his head, danced to the music.
But, paralyzed from the neck down,
the rest of his body did not.
Yet a dancer can recognize a dancer,
and I found him sensual and sexy.

Forgive me, God, for not asking him to dance.
He was in a wheelchair,
    but that wasn't my reason.
Stairs separated us,
    but that wasn't my reason.
He was with a friend,
    but that wasn't my reason.
My "reason" was:
    I didn't want to seem patronizing,
asking him to dance.
Now I realize it was equally patronizing
not to ask!
God, forgive me;
I didn't know what to do.

*   *   *

She's in a wheelchair, God.
She wants a woman to love her.
Friends love her.
They don't let the wheelchair get in the way.
They're liberal and politically correct.
They're also genuinely good people.
But she wants a woman to *love* her,
to love *all of her,*
    even the parts that are numb.

And she wants to love a woman
        with *all that she is,*
paralyzed parts and all!

Dear God, send her a lover.
Give her someone who loves all of her
and who can receive all of her love.
For her disability is found
neither in her love nor in her lovemaking
(in these areas she has more ability
        than most),
but in our physical perfectionism.

DAY 33

O Creator,
we glorify your name
and enjoy you forever.
You have immersed us in your world
and baptized us with your Spirit.

We see your beauty reflected
in our community and in your creation:
We enjoy you forever.

We feel your love in the warmth of sun,
the smiles of strangers,
the hugs of friends,
the bodies of lovers:
We enjoy you forever.

We taste your refreshment
of sleep, of breath,
of food and drink:
We enjoy you forever.

We smell your fragrance
of flower and field,
of flesh and flavor:
We enjoy you forever.

We hear your voice
from the winds of nature
to the winds of spirit:
We enjoy you forever.

O Creator, open our eyes
so we may see your goodness.
Sensitize our numbed senses

so we may feel your goodness.
Overcome our blandness
so we may taste your goodness.
Break into our vacuum
so we may smell your goodness.
Unstop our ears
so we may hear your goodness.

O Creator, our Creator,
we glorify your name
and enjoy you forever.
Alleluia!

DAY 34

Holy Mother and Father of us all,
people around Jesus saw the heavens open,
and the Spirit descend as a dove,
and heard a voice from heaven say,
"You are my beloved Child;
with you I am well pleased."

How lesbian and gay youth
would love to hear these words, O God!
From you, their heavenly mother and father;
from earthly mothers and fathers,
    their parents;
from spiritual mothers and fathers,
    their church:
"You are our beloved children;
with you we are well pleased."

We pray for them in their growth:
knowing themselves,
finding our community,
meeting significant others
in a world infected by AIDS,
in a culture disabled by heterosexism,
in a church sick with homophobia.

We pray for an ignorant world:
the culture and the church that wonder
why youth run away or are cast aside,
why so many teen suicides,
why drugs and alcohol cloud young minds,
why apparently happy, successful youth
choose death in various forms
    rather than life.

We pray for lesbian and gay youth
who suffer external and internal violence:
for those who are visible and often suffer
physical and verbal attacks,
ridicule by peers and adults,
last choice for teams, friendships,
       and parties;
for those who are invisible and often suffer
inward torment that,
despite their achievements,
no one would love them if they knew.

We pray for young lesbians and gay men
searching for public and personal
       role models,
but too frequently offered
people with whom they can't identify,
while those with whom they might identify
are the least visible and available.

As you identified yourself with your Child,
       O God,
may we stand in solidarity
       with our gay sons and daughters,
saying, "You are our beloved children;
with you we are well pleased."

DAY 35

God of every color,
the one whose words and manner
made me want to speak and write
with gentle, eloquent significance
was black.
Yet, though he was principal
    of my high school,
his family was not allowed
to buy a home in our neighborhood.

God of every color and ethnicity,
the ones whose passionate purpose
inspired my social activism
with passion and purpose
were black and brown and yellow and white,
Jewish, Central American, Vietnamese,
    and black South African.
Yet, though spiritual and political leaders,
they were poor, exploited, fired from jobs,
    disfranchised,
imprisoned, embattled, tortured,
    and martyred.

God, forgive us.
God, deliver us.
For we have accepted the gifts of many
while rejecting their body-selves
because of color, ethnicity, gender, age,
disability, sexual orientation, appearance.

Help us to celebrate another's value
by the fruits,
not the shape of the tree.

DAY 36

O Holy One,
I don't want to go to church today.
It's a beautiful day to be outside.
I've got so many things to do.
I need a day to myself.
Nobody will miss me.

But I will miss me, God.
I keep forgetting
that I go to church for myself,
not for other people,
not even for you, God,
though I would piously like to think so.
You don't need me to fill a pew,
but I need you to fill my heart
with reminders of your best hopes for me,
for our community,
for the world.

I can't understand spirituality alone.
Often it's too enigmatic or amorphous.
From icon to scripture to saint to sacrament:
"You have to be there," I guess,
         to understand.

O Holy One,
help me to "be there,"
to stand with them,
those from scripture and tradition
who enjoyed your presence,
and those in the church and community
who enjoy your presence

in the midst of their experience,
in the midst of our experience.

Show me the window or the door,
not to look in as spiritual voyeur,
but to enter as spiritual participant,
a member of your family,
your child,
among sisters and brothers in faith.
Amen.

DAY 37

Cosmic Lover of us all,
who provides rain and sun for all,
we follow your lead by praying
for those who oppose us.

We pray for those
who have set themselves against us
    in the church,
claiming we don't belong,
while we affirm we all belong.

We join them in their prayers:
that scripture be upheld—
its liberating power and its loving power;
that biblical models of mercy, sacrifice,
    and steadfastness
may inform all of our relationships;
that the gift of the Spirit might be given
    to all,
so we may better discern your presence
    in one another;
that their opposing viewpoints be heard,
so we may better listen
to one another's spiritual experience.

May a love affair with the Bible,
steadfast mercy toward one another,
receptiveness to the Spirit,
and an ear to diverse viewpoints
continue the reformation of the church.

We pray for those
who have set themselves against us
    in the culture,

claiming we have no rights,
while we affirm everyone's rights.

We join them in their hopes:
that political and social values
        will be upheld—
right to privacy and equal protection
        under the law;
that societal models of justice
        and compassion
will inform all of our cultural institutions;
that the gift of liberty may be available to all
so we may exercise our rights and privileges;
that their questions and concerns be heard,
so we may better listen
        to one another's experience.

May a love affair with societal values,
concern for justice and compassion,
freedom for individuals and groups,
and democratic diversity
continue the reformation of society.

Lover of all,
may the church and culture
follow your lead in equitable treatment.
Amen.

DAY 38

God,
how did Abraham and Sarah feel
when you called them
from their comfortable home
to an unknown promised land?

How did the spouses of Matthew or Mary feel
when Jesus called these disciples
from their homes
to teach them about love?

God,
how do married couples feel
when one acknowledges being gay
and they choose to continue the journey
    together?

Or how do wives or husbands feel
whose beloved gay spouses leave them
to learn more about love?

These are not easy choices.
They involve pain and sacrifice,
patience and understanding,
stamina and a resolute spirit.

God,
be with today's Abraham and Sarah,
today's wife of Matthew,
and today's husband of Mary,
either called into uncharted territory
or called to let go.

God,
these are often your calls

to people of faith;
yet you promise to be with them
in the wilderness
and in exile
until a promised land is found
and reconciliation is possible.

DAY 39

Mother God, Father God,
bless parents of lesbians and gay men
as they come out of the closet individually,
and organizationally in chapters of
Parents and Friends of Lesbians and Gays.

As you came out of the safety of heaven
    with Jesus,
may parents of lesbians and gay men come out.
In Immanuel, God-with-us,
you also came out of a womb
    of perceived scandal,
out of a wilderness of temptations,
and out of a humiliating closet-tomb,
to communicate your love and grace and
    mercy.

As you were one with your Child,
may parents feel one with their own flesh
    and blood
who are gay and lesbian.
As you yourself were crucified in Jesus,
may parents of gay children
understand themselves crucified
by homophobia, heterosexism, and AIDS.

As you supported your Child
by gloriously trumpeting his birth,
by ministering to him in his wilderness,
by shaking the earth at his death,
so may parents support gay children
by celebrating their coming out,
ministering to them in the dry places,

and grieving at all the deaths
    they experience.

As you vindicated your Child
    through resurrection,
so may parents bring new life
by reconciling with gay daughters and sons,
by championing their quest for rights
    and opportunities,
by contending with those who would crucify
    them,
by welcoming their children's joys and loves
    and laughter.

We pray for parents in their struggles:
struggles for information,
struggles toward affirmation,
struggles with those who sit in judgment
of themselves and their children.
May they remember you have suffered
    with them.
May they also view your own coming out
    with Jesus
as your identification and support,
vindication and resurrection
with, for, and of them.

DAY 40

Holy Friend,
surrounded by the carnage of AIDS
we know the shock, horror, disbelief,
denial, anger, hurt, fear, terror,
and loneliness
the disciples felt
as they mourned the death
of their young, idealistic friend
named Jesus.

You too, his holy Parent,
appeared to briefly turn your back
    on his suffering,
you felt it so keenly.
You know my feelings.
Prayer is the only place I may bring
    my feelings
and know I'm fully understood.
A therapist, a spiritual advisor, a pastor,
a lover, family, friends
only know in part.
But in prayer I am fully known,
and in prayer I may more fully understand.

So here I am.
In this silent place, lead me to understand—
not why so many friends have died with AIDS,
not why the friend of humanity, Jesus, died,
but, rather, what is the meaning
    of their deaths for me?
What transformation is called for in myself
by their blood, like Abel's,

crying out from earth's soil?
In the light of your Spirit, O God,
lead me to discern the needed transformation.
By the power of your Spirit, O God,
enable me to carry out that transformation.
Otherwise, for me, their deaths will be
    in vain,
their souls will not rest,
and there will be no resurrection.
May prayer transform me this day, O God,
that I may experience resurrection firsthand.

You speak to me in scripture:
the women, on their way to minister
    to his body,
found Jesus alive.
The disciples, praying together,
found him alive.
Two disciples, sharing a meal
    with a stranger,
found him alive.
In ministry, in prayer, in sharing
    with strangers,
may I too find Christ alive.
And may I find those
    who have gone before me
into unending communion with you, God.
Thank you, holy Friend. Alleluia! Amen.

CITIZENS
OF A
COMMONWEALTH

A snail stretched its full length in a strenuous assault, climbing the tall picture window. Inside, those of us on retreat discussed our visions of the future church. A sadness had slipped into some hearts, as often happens the final day of a retreat. The common purpose, camaraderie, and caring intimacy that are experienced at such gatherings inevitably lead one to wonder, Why can't it always be like this? Our visions of hope for the church painfully reminded us of our place—or lack thereof—in the present church, intensifying our letdown. Yes, we were on the downhill side of our mountaintop experience. Yet the slowly ascending snail, apparently unintimidated by the long vertical climb, offered hope for progress.

The closing worship pulled us together one last time and lifted our spirits. Singing songs, reflecting on scripture, offering prayers, and sharing communion unified us not only with one another, but with unseen others dead and living, unseen others within the church, and unseen others who have left the church. Worship served as a witness to the resurrection while it celebrated with thanksgiving the brief life of this gathering of lesbian and gay Christians, our families and friends.

Lesbian and gay Christians and those who love us have discovered that God has given us a special grace, a unique charism, to offer the broader church. Having been treated like strangers, we know better how to make others feel welcomed. Our hugs become a sacrament of God's embodied love for Christians who are afraid to touch one another. Our ability to listen compassionately serves Christians who are afraid to express their emotional and sexual feelings. Our passion for justice prophetically troubles a church embarrassed by passion and fearful of conflict. The intimacy and celebration that characterize our worship reflect how, facing rejection, we developed a trust in the most intimate lover of us all: God. Our ability to party well helps all Christians enjoy the grace of God which embraces us.

Yet perhaps the most welcome gift God has given lesbian and gay Christians as marginalized people, as well as those marginalized with us because of their love and support, is our high hopes for the church and the cultures in which we live. It is our vision of God's spiritual commonwealth that gives us the stamina, the chutzpah, and the hope to keep the faith despite naysayers within the church and within the gay and feminist communities. We believe that lesbians and gay men are also children of God, heirs with Christ of a realm over which God is sovereign. Our vision makes us attractive to many Christians who have lost the liberating vision of an inbreaking kingdom, or commonwealth, of God. People watch the lesbian and gay Christian movement in amazement, just as I watched that snail climbing the picture window at the retreat. Where does it think it's going? they might wonder. God knows.

On our way to God's commonwealth, like the snail, we find there are dry places that are difficult to slide past, let alone climb beyond. We miss the smoother places where we seem to glide: retreats, conferences, and other gatherings. Many are not able to benefit from these opportunities for communion. Most lesbians, gays, our families, and our friends do not have regular access to support groups, supportive and integrated congregations, or gay and lesbian congregations. Many rarely experience worship in which gay sexuality finds its proper place as occasion for both confession and thanksgiving. They rarely enjoy spiritual community in which lesbian sexuality serves as an opportunity for support and celebration. These return to their home churches from retreats such as ours having tasted God's commonwealth, glad to know it exists *somewhere* and *sometime,* but wishing for its availability every day.

I believe that prayer offers us access to that commonwealth. Daily prayer means we can experience communion with lesbian and gay Christians—and all gays of faith—every day. Prayer offers community between gay and nongay, and among all those who love and support lesbian women and gay men: families, friends, advocates. We share one another's suffering and we share one another's glory. "If one member suffers, all suffer together; if one member is honored, all rejoice together" (1 Cor. 12:26).

Prayer also empowers us to uphold our vision of God's commonwealth: a vision of the present— gay, bisexual, and straight in solidarity together; and a vision of the future—the recognition and celebration that God's common spiritual wealth has been bestowed upon all.

And in prayer we hear God's call from mere contemplation of this commonwealth to living (as scripture says) "as if" it were already here, thus acting on behalf of all who are marginalized, disfranchised, and oppressed by the church or culture. I believe that it is in saying and living our prayers that we most readily experience the commonwealth of God in our midst.

DAY 41

It's so easy to say prayers, God,
so difficult to translate our words to
        actions.
Your Word became flesh and dwelt among us.
We nailed him,
we suffocated him,*
we buried him,
in part because we were so damned jealous
that he did something we couldn't:
he lived out his prayer life.
When he prayed "Thy kingdom come"
he meant it,
he preached it,
he lived as its citizen
and became its King.
We mocked him
by making his throne a cross
because we thought he mocked us,
making it seem so easy to be your children,
        God.
Though tempted as we are,
he, in prayer and fasting,
waited on your word,
refused to tempt your love,
and worshiped only you.**

O God,
forgive me for not waiting,

---

*Crucifixion works by eventually strangling its victim. The
body sags from exhaustion and cuts off the flow of air to the
lungs.
**See Jesus' temptation story in Matthew 4:1-11.

forgive me for tempting you,
forgive my worship of idols.
Teach me to listen for your word,
trust in your love,
and worship in spirit and in truth.
Remind me that Jesus is not an only child,
nor your kingdom's only citizen.
May I live up to my inheritance as your child
and as a citizen of your commonwealth,
through Jesus Christ, who leads my way.
Amen.

DAY 42

You who chose the weak
"to shame the strong":
we pray for the especially vulnerable.
We pray for lesbians and gays
      already marginalized
by color of skin, gender,
economic or educational poverty,
age.

We pray for Black, Latino, and Asian
      gays and lesbians,
who often face homophobic communities
and who face a homophobic and racist
      church.

We pray for lesbian women,
especially in the church,
whose vulnerability and resulting fear
even gay men cannot comprehend.

We pray for gay people who are poor,
economically or educationally,
whose financial insecurity
or lack of knowledge
limits their ability to affirm themselves,
assert and articulate their needs,
let alone benefit from participation
      in gay communities.

We pray for lesbians and gays
who are very young or very old,
who live at home with families
or in retirement homes with strangers,

where sexuality is frequently ignored
     or suppressed
and access to gay family is limited.

You who have chosen the especially vulnerable
to proclaim your word
   and your commonwealth:
remind the church of its call
as a community of the vulnerable,
welcoming self-disclosure,
celebrating your affirmation,
embodying your presence in the world,
which transforms shepherds to kings,
elderly couples to parents,
unwed mothers to saints,
questioning youth to rabbis,
poor fishermen to spiritual leaders,
legalistic persecutors to preachers
     of God's grace,
vulnerable followers to visionaries.

Empower the especially vulnerable, today,
with visions of your grace.
Amen.

DAY 43

"What is the chief end of [humanity]?
To glorify God, and to enjoy [God] forever."*
And what is *your* chief end, O God?
To glorify *us,* and enjoy *us* forever?

Isn't this heretical? At least presumptuous?
Forgive me, God, if I've wrongly described
    your agenda.
But, from the day you made us cocreators
    in Adam and Eve
to the day you made us heirs with Christ,
it seems you've been sharing your glory
and enjoying our participation in it.

Our courtship was rocky:
    we kept running from you,
    dating others less worthy,
    pursuing selfish desires
    and our greedy lusts.
Finally, you moved in with us in Jesus,
    became our lover,
    saved us from destruction
    and gave up your life for us.
Now we're haunted by your Ghost,
    who brings us together,
        different as we are,
    reconciling us one with another
        and with you.

---

*From the Westminster Shorter Catechism, in *The Book of Confessions,* Part I of the *Constitution of the Presbyterian Church (U.S.A.),* 7.001.

"The world is charged with the glory of God"
(to slightly modify Gerard Manley Hopkins's
          line).
So are we, because you have visited us,
and our faces shine with the Shekinah,
          your glory,
that lit up Moses' face and made him
          veil himself.
Why are we afraid to lift the veil
and show ourselves and the world
the glorious riches of our spiritual
          inheritance?

God, help us lift the veil,
removing all that obscures your glory
          graciously given
in our creation, redemption, and inspiration.
By so doing, may we glorify you,
our glorifier in heaven,
and enjoy you forever.
Amen.

DAY 44

(Dedicated to the memory of Lyle Loder)

Dear God,
friends with AIDS
slip through my fingers
faster than grains of sand,
and seemingly as many.

I can't hold them.

God, dear God,
please catch them
with your open hands,
within your welcoming embrace,
with your loving heart.

I wish I could be there for them.

I pray they'll be there for me
when I slip.
You too, my God,
our God.
Amen.

DAY 45

Holy Creator,
thank you for artists:
visual, verbal,
musical, kinesthetic,
spiritual.

Holy Creator,
thank you for artists
who express our impressions,
our feelings, and our hopes.

Your gospel is found
not only in scripture,
but in the stroke of a brush
or of a pen,
in melody and harmony and dissonance,
within dance and movement,
within prayer.

Bless the prophecy of artists
who charm and chide,
critique and cajole,
who prompt tears, laughter,
peace, and passion.

Within their creative process
may we recognize
the divine in all creation
and be moved to awe
and wonder and worship.

Receive all art, O Divine Creator,
as acts of prayer,

a reflection and response
of creation.
And, as the disciples requested,
continue to "teach us to pray."
Amen.

DAY 46

Dear Jesus,
sometimes we expect too much sanctuary
within the church.
We want a womb,
a warm, retreat experience,
not harsh reality
of needy people
and petty politics,
ecclesiastical or societal,
which may lead to a tomb
as it did for you.

But the kingdom of heaven lay beyond
your forty-day prayer retreat
    in the wilderness, Jesus.
The commonwealth of God lay within
your interactions with the world
    that followed.

The commonwealth you preached, Jesus,
is in our midst
as healing occurs among us.
And healing comes
as you, the Christ, are in the world,
not in retreat,
nor entombed
either by calcified doctrines
or grave doubt.

You taught that for us to pray,
for us to find healing for ourselves,
is not enough.
"Faith without works is dead."

Faith without work is death.
Dear Jesus,
keep me from resting in peace,
a self-satisfied smile on my face,
while others hunger for my touch
as a member of your Body,
the Body of Christ,
healer of this world.
Amen.

DAY 47

God, we confess that we confuse
sexuality and power, love and control,
in church, in society, in relationship.

Forgive us when we dominate, intimidate,
abuse, exploit, or try to control others
verbally, physically, emotionally,
     spiritually.

Redeem us from being forced to submission,
from being abused and exploited
     and controlled
by the church, by the government, by lovers.

As you called the paralytic to walk,
lift us from the paralysis of low self-esteem
so we may walk into your commonwealth
with the power you have given us:
a power we do not need to prove
     by lording it over others,
a power we do not have to sacrifice
     to love you or others.

In crucifixion,
you gave up power as the world knows power:
domination, control, and exploitation.
In resurrection,
you revealed the power of your spiritual
     commonwealth:
choosing love, choosing life, choosing unity.

Resurrect us, God; call us to rise
     and carry our pallets,

and let religious and political leaders
    and friends alike
stand amazed at our healing,
and with those of long ago who witnessed
    the paralytic walk,
may they witness in us your power and glory:
a power which seeks not to dominate
    but to serve,
a glory which seeks not itself
    but others.

Then may they also glorify you, saying,
"We never saw anything like this."

DAY 48

Sovereign of the commonwealth that is
    and will be:
more than forty wars are being fought
    in your world today.
Your peoples spend a million dollars
    per minute
preparing and engaging in war.
Your world is embarrassed
by sexual and spiritual passions,
yet this passion for war
is displayed daily on television and radio
and in newspapers and magazines.

Give us, O Sovereign,
your passion for peace and peacemaking.
You are leading us from the precipice
    of nuclear holocaust.
Deliver us also from peace without justice,
    another form of violence.
Engage us in a love affair with human rights.
Convert our budgets and priorities
    to meet human needs,
        especially hunger, malnutrition, disease,
        and ignorance.
Redirect our economies
    to share the world's goods and resources
        equitably.
Make us better stewards of your creation.

May the vision of your commonwealth,
    O Sovereign,
transform us,

so that we are willing to go the extra mile,
to give not only our coat, but our cloak
    as well,
even risk crucifixion—
all for the sake of justice and mercy,
the things which make for peace.
Amen.

DAY 49

"Dust thou art,
and unto dust shalt thou return."

Eternal One,
it's not so much that life is short;
it's that there seems to be so little time
    for life!
Chores, work, obligations, meetings,
    business—
it's a wonder we have time left.
An average person spends a year of life
    brushing teeth!
Where's the time
for creating, re-creating, and loving
that we value so highly as life?

Eternal One,
maybe my approach to the job of life
blinds me to its joy.
Restore my sight that I may see
my chores, work, obligations, meetings,
    and business
as opportunities for creating, re-creating,
    and loving.
But if, despite my newfound vision,
I discover some of these get in the way
of living my life abundantly,
give me courage
to dispense with the superfluous,
abandon the hopeless,

and leap over roadblocks,
so that I may more fully embrace life.

Eternal One,
inspire me to redeem my time in this way.

DAY 50

God of Yes:
to the physically challenged,
to the mentally handicapped,
we, the church, have said both yes and no:
Yes, come to church.
No, we have no wheelchair ramps.
No, we have no signers.
No, we don't want seizures interrupting
    worship.
No, we don't have the time or patience
to wait for you to articulate your insights
    in meetings.

God of Yes:
how much more of a "no" is heard
if the differently-abled person is lesbian
    or gay!
It's said the hearing-impaired have
    a gay ratio
twice that of the general population.
Is this true of other disabilities?
No matter, God,
because the sexuality of the disabled,
no matter how "normal,"
is almost as taboo in the church
as homosexuality.

God, in your Child, Jesus Christ,
your embodied "yes" to us
    disabled by a cross:
challenge the church's disabilities,
particularly our ambivalence.

In Christ, help us to embody a hearty yes
to those challenged by physical or mental
       boundaries.
In Christ, help us to embody a hearty yes
to their spirituality and sexuality.

In Christ, may we feel the healing touch
of the hearty yes of their embodiment,
creating access for Christ's Body
into a new embassy of reconciliation.

As that Body, we pray. Amen.

DAY 51

For white-haired ladies in the church
who ardently defend gay and lesbian rights
as they have always defended women's rights:
Thanks, God!

For Bible-believing fundamentalists
who, faithful to the Spirit's leading,
recognize her presence in gay Christians:
Thanks, God!

For social gospel liberals,
progressive politically,
    but personally conservative,
whose agenda now includes sexual justice:
Thanks, God!

For those who work for, lobby for, vote for
the repeal of antigay laws,
and the end of antigay law enforcement,
and the passage of gay civil rights legislation:
Thanks, God!

For those who work for, lobby for, vote for
protection of the rights of persons
    infected with HIV
and adequate funding for AIDS research,
    treatment, and care:
Thanks, God!

For those who work for, lobby for, vote for
a change in the church's negative stance
    on homosexuality,

particularly its ban on ordination
    of lesbians and gay men:
Thanks, God!

For those who offer information, education,
    and models,
for healing our phobias related to sexuality
    and homosexuality,
and bringing integrity of spirituality
    and sexuality:
Thanks, God!

For those who promote and enforce laws
    against gay-bashing,
whether by young drunken men
    or by older bigoted legislators,
as violence against us increases
    in the AIDS crisis:
Thanks, God!

For those who have risked their lives,
    careers, and standing
(No greater love has anyone than this,
    Jesus said)
for the sake of our cause in the church
    and the culture:
Thanks, God!

For those who endure enormous ignorance
    and hostility,
countless meetings and phone calls
    and endless paper shuffling,

to accomplish the historic work
    of your commonwealth:
Thanks, God!

For the "so great a cloud of witnesses"
    which surrounds us,
"with people of faith from all times
    and places"* who confess
that blessed are *all* those
    who come "in the name of the Lord":
Thanks, God!

---

*From the Communion liturgy.

DAY 52

You washed our feet, Jesus.
At first we objected,
but you made it clear that to be part of you
we need first to receive your gifts
and serve others the same way.

You gave us bread and wine, Jesus.
We took it for granted,
not realizing what it meant to you,
how it meant flesh and blood,
unity with you and with one another
and salvation for the world.

You said we would betray and deny you, Jesus.
"Not me!" we each cried,
but we all did
in our own way,
leaving you to face your destiny alone.

You asked us to pray with you, Jesus.
We fell asleep
and missed sharing your anguish,
not being compassionate to the Compassionate;
then they took you from us.

You continue to love us, Jesus.
We object, we take it for granted,
we betray and deny you,
and sleep
instead of pray.

Forgive us, Jesus,
for we know not what we do.

DAY 53

She's angry, Mother God,
and sometimes it feels as though
she's angry with *me*.
As a lesbian woman,
she feels the pain of being twice denied
by her church.

Mother God, vessel her anger:
may it purge and purify the place
    you choose to dwell.
Mother God, shield her and those near her,
that the fire of her rage
    may not be all-consuming,
but liberating for us all.

Mother God, when will Christians understand
women have been cut off from their own
    spirituality
by rational theologians, church patriarchy,
and false, exclusively male images of you?
Many fear women's spirituality. But why?
Has it not helped shape Christianity
    for two millennia?

Mother God, bless women as they intentionally
and consciously assert their spirituality.
May women and men be moved
    by feminist insights
leading to a more intuitive, feeling-full,
embodied, and earth-centered spirituality;
a communal ecclesiology;
icons inclusive of your feminine nature;

and transformed visions of your future
    as commonwealth
rather than as feudal, patriarchal,
    and parochial kingdom.

Mother God,
carry us upon your earthen hip,
and dandle us upon your cosmic knees.

DAY 54

God,
you've been very, very good to me!
I sometimes marvel that
things have come together
as well as they have.

And yet, it's when things are going well
I forget your telephone number.
I don't reach out
and give you thanks.

With the ten lepers who begged your attention
for healing of their leprosy and isolation,
I cry to you when troubled:
"Mommy, kiss it and make it better!"
"Daddy, fix this for me!"

And with the ten lepers Jesus healed,
nine times out of ten,
when things are going well again,
I don't return to your presence,
or I take your presence for granted.

May I join the lone leper who did return
to give you thanks,
that one Samaritan despised by others
but loved by you.

Thank you, God,
in Jesus Christ
through your Holy Spirit.
Amen.

DAY 55

Merciful God, for me
the most moving entry in this year's
gay and lesbian pride parade
was that of an AIDS hospice.
The parade's theme, "Look to the Future,"
inspired their float:
a house, their AIDS hospice,
with a "For Sale" sign out front.

Merciful God,
tears come to my eyes as I imagine the day
when AIDS hospices and services
will no longer be needed,
when death will no longer have
    its special sting,
taking the lives of so many so young.

Merciful God,
keep this vision of your commonwealth
    before us:
a time when there will be a cure,
a treatment, a vaccine,
adequate to the task of destroying HIV
and its ability to ravage a body
and our community
and the world.

Merciful God,
in the AIDS crisis, many of us have learned:
how attentive society must be to the health
    needs of sexual and racial minorities—
    not just those of the mainstream,

how equitably health care must be provided
    to the poor,
how necessary a global view is
    in providing health care,
    particularly within the Third World,
how vital international cooperation is
    in medical research,
how valuable making one's own decisions
    about one's body is,
how healing the touch of a loved one can be,
how powerful is the human spirit,
how necessary is our spirituality.
Thank you for creating us as explorers
who, in the midst of suffering,
discover dimensions of your commonwealth.

Merciful God,
as we await our vision of an AIDS-free world,
lead us to discern the paths that lead to life.
In our lovemaking, keep us safe.
In our caregiving, protect us from burnout.
In our health-keeping, help us
    to reduce stress, exercise properly,
    nourish ourselves adequately,
    and find appropriate care and treatment.
May we live to see your day
    when AIDS is vanquished,
and enjoy the inevitable, glorious,
    global party!
Alleluia! Amen!

DAY 56

"Hosanna in the highest!"
"Blessed is the one who comes in the name
  of the Lord!"

When people cried these words,
Jesus said if the crowds had been silent,
the very stones would have cried out.

"Blessed is the one who comes in the name
  of the Lord!"

Will anyone ever say this of me, O God?
Will I ever become the disciple,
  the Christ-bearer,
who will make people feel blessed
  by your presence
when I am with them?

"Take my life, and let it be
  consecrated, Lord, to thee."
God, I pray these words from an old hymn
  as a prayer.
I too wish people to feel your presence
  through me.
Yet do I understand the implications
  of this prayer?
Aren't I like James and John
  wishing for glory
rather than sharing Christ's cup of suffering
as their mother did by following him
  to the cross?
And, God, as it was for Simon Peter

when he refused to believe that Jesus
    would suffer,
aren't my expectations of what it means
to be your presence in the world false?
Isn't everyone's expectation
    of what it means
to be God's presence in the world false?
Isn't that why we, the world,
    crucified Jesus?

Yet Simon Peter's mother-in-law
    got your message:
healed from a fever, she served others.
You, our spiritual Sovereign,
come to us as a suffering Servant,
demonstrating that spiritual greatness depends
on our willingness to serve.

I want the joy of your commonwealth,
but am unwilling to go through the poverty,
    peril, and pain
of the transformation required
    to experience it.

O God, forgive me.
Disarm my expectations.
Lead me in transformation
as a citizen of your commonwealth,
that I might better be your presence
    in the world.

DAY 57

Dear God,
we spend a lot of time praying—
on bar stools, drink in hand,
at parties, dressed just right,
during fund-raisers, politically correct,
in service organizations, volunteering—
praying for Mr. or Ms. Right to come along!

Dear God,
may my life become an opportunity for me
to become the right person
rather than simply to look for the right person;
to become all those things I value
in you, God, and in others.

Help me sweep my house clean
to find the lost silver coin within,
as did the woman of Jesus' parable.

May I prove unafraid to use and develop
the talents you have given me,
as did the good and faithful servants.

Don't let me sink back in fear,
either of failure or of success.
Jesus experienced both:
crucifixion, resurrection.
Had he been paralyzed by fear of either,
I might not be praying this prayer.

And finally, dear God,
in looking for the right person,

may I avoid the mistake
of the forgiven servant
who proved unforgiving.
Amen.

DAY 58

"Love never ends;
as for prophecies, they will pass away;
as for tongues, they will cease;
as for knowledge, it will pass away.
So faith, hope, love abide, these three;
but the greatest of these is love."

Lovemaking God,
God who is love,
this scripture puts everything
    in perspective.

We struggle to be prophets,
to speak meaningfully,
to gain and share knowledge,
but our efforts must always be surpassed,
as "new occasions teach new duties."*

We struggle to keep faith and hope alive,
yet faith and hope are forever
a part of the human experience.

Our most important and valuable and eternal
    struggle
is to give and to receive love.
May we recognize your eternal presence
in all that is done for love
and give you thanks.
Amen.

---

*From the hymn "Once to Every One and Nation"; words by
James Russell Lowell.

DAY 59

O God, deliver us.

From anger we turn inward
or misdirect toward those we love,
deliver us.

From wanting our opponents' downfall
rather than their liberation,
deliver us.

From fear, anxiety, stress, or loneliness
that makes us seek a quick fix
of religious or political absolutes,
of drugs or alcohol,
of compulsive sexual expression,
or "messianic" lover,
O God, deliver us.

From believing what "they" say about us,
devaluing ourselves or others like us,
deliver us.

From lack of trust and faith
in ourselves as individuals
and ourselves as community,
O God, deliver us.

From lack of commitment
to lover, to friends,
to our faith, to our community,
deliver us.

From denial of our integrity
as spiritual-sexual creations,
deliver us.

From rejection of others
because of their body-state,
whether gender, race, age,
sexual orientation,
appearance, or disability,
O God, deliver us.

Free us to live your commonwealth, O God.
Clarify our vision,
purify our motives,
renew our hope.
In the name of you who create us,
of the Christ who calls us,
of the Spirit who empowers us,
we pray, O God. Amen.

DAY 60

We are hungry for love, God:
feed us.

We are thirsty for justice, God:
give us to drink.

We are naked in our vulnerability, God:
clothe us protectively.

We are imprisoned by prejudice, God:
liberate us.

We are sick and dying, God:
comfort us.

We are strangers and alone, God:
offer us a home.

Who will perform this ministry?

Those to whom Jesus the Christ will say:
"Come, O blessed of God,
inherit the commonwealth
prepared for you
from the foundation of the world."
Amen and amen.

EPILOGUE

Hebrew scriptures tell a wonderful story about how earthly life was saved from death by Noah's ark. They also record how the Hebrews chose life by Israel's covenant of the Mosaic law, a written law that was contained in the Ark of the Covenant. When Christians experienced and understood a new covenant with God through Jesus Christ, the church was symbolized as the ark of a new covenant by which all life would be saved, this time through the transforming waters of baptism rather than through the destructive waters of a flood.

When I think of the institutional church these days, however, images of death come to me rather than images of life. I'm not sure why. Maybe it's because I believe that, in some sense, the church would prefer death for those of us who are lesbian and gay, or at least the equivalent of death: a casket-sized closet. Maybe it's because I believe that the church too often chooses death for itself:

159

by rigidity, by exclusivity, by stupidity, by insensitivity. It too often closets itself in a world hungry for political liberation, societal revitalization, and spiritual community. The church has frequently seemed like those whitewashed tombs Jesus decried: outwardly they "appear beautiful, but within they are full of dead men's bones and all uncleanness," outwardly they "appear righteous . . . , but within . . . are full of hypocrisy and iniquity" (Matt. 23:27–28).

In contrast, when I consider the gay and lesbian community facing the AIDS crisis in the midst of pervasive homophobia and heterosexism, images of life come to me. It seems ironic, since we have experienced more and more death through this modern-day plague. But we have also witnessed the indomitable human spirit in persons living with AIDS and in persons who have died from AIDS. We have been surrounded by saints who have sacrificially served as professional and volunteer caregivers. We have seen lovers, friends, and families who have ministered to their loved ones in their hours of need. We have witnessed social justice advocates lobbying societal institutions for just and fair treatment, civil rights, adequate education, research, and care. We are more aware of the glory of life in the present and more open to life beyond death. We know that our love transcends bodily existence while still embracing it.

I believe that if one were to look within our community with eyes of faith, one would see the suffering and the resurrected Christ, the compassionate and the healing Christ, the struggling and the victorious Christ. At the doors of too many churches, angels would warn us, "Christ is not here. Christ has risen. Why do you seek the living among the dead? Christ goes before you into the gay and lesbian community." Together with the *campesinos* of Central America, blacks of South Africa, women throughout the world, people of faith in the emerging democracies of Eastern Europe, and others, we serve as a new ark of a spirituality that is liberating, life-giving, love-affirming, and justice-seeking.

Just as all species of life were saved by the faith of Noah, so our spirituality may prove salvific for more than ourselves. Our spirituality's ability to embrace sexuality may lead to spiritual-sexual integrity in our religious communities. And just as Sodom could have been saved had ten righteous persons been found, so the church may be saved of its Sodomlike inhospitality by the leavening presence of lesbian and gay Christians and our families and friends. For, as I have written in other places, I believe that ultimately the church's inability to accept lesbians and gay men is a spiritual problem. If the church could become more inclusive in its prayer life—inclusive of sexuality in its several expressions—its membership and ministry would naturally become inclusive of us. Spirituality may serve as common ground on which we come out to one another as people of faith. Through prayer, the Spirit of God may redeem our common ground as holy ground. Then, I believe,

> "Steadfast love and faithfulness will meet;
> righteousness and peace will kiss
> each other." (Ps. 85:10)

INDEX: Scripture References in Prayers

Index of Scripture

INDEX OF TOPICS

Citations correspond to the day of the prayer.

Index of Topics

Index of Topics